My Bi
Brother Ned

by Jeff Allen
illustrated by Peggy Tagel

HOUGHTON MIFFLIN BOSTON

Printed in India

ISBN-13: 978-0-547-01863-8
ISBN-10: 0-547-01863-0

2 3 4 5 6 7 8 9 0940 15 14 13 12 11 10

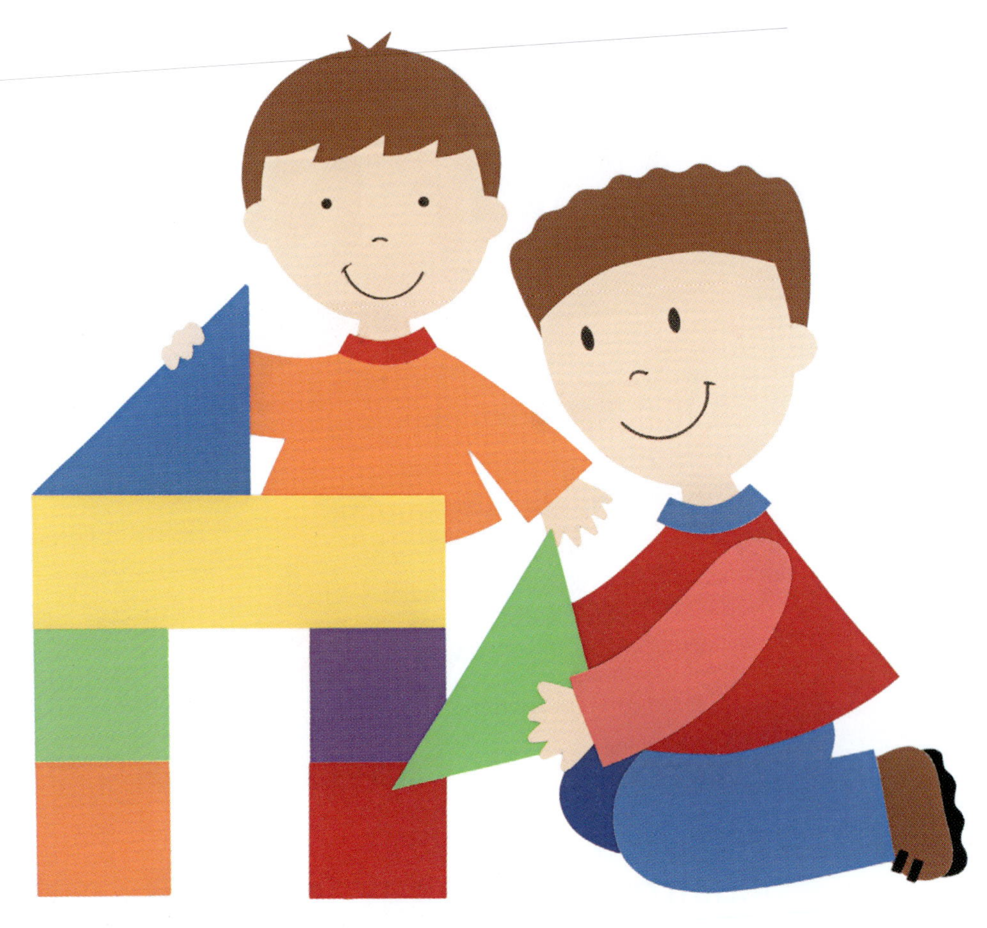

Ned can build a house with me.

Ned can bake a cake
with me.

Ned can paint a picture with me.

Ned can read a book with me.

Ned can play a game with me!

Responding

TARGET SKILL **Compare and Contrast** This story is about two brothers. How are they alike or not? Make a diagram.

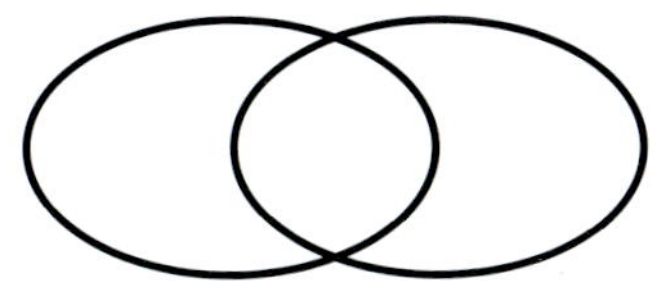

Write About It

Text to Self Draw two pictures. Show a friend or family member in one picture and you in the other. Write a sentence telling how you are alike or not.

have | **help**

TARGET SKILL **Compare and Contrast** Tell how two things are alike or not.

TARGET STRATEGY **Monitor/Clarify** Find ways to figure out what doesn't make sense.

GENRE **Realistic fiction** is a story that could happen in real life.